Olive Oil

A cultural history from around the world

Ed S. Milton

Astrolog Publishing House Ltd.

Edited by: S. Milton
Cover Design: Na'ama Yaffe
Layout and Graphics: Daniel Akerman

P.O. Box 1123, Hod Hasharon 45111, Israel
Tel: 972-9-7412044
Fax: 972-9-7442714

ISBN 965-494-160-0

Published by Astrolog Publishing House 2003

10 9 8 7 6 5 4 3 2 1

n a book about the vitamins and minerals that are necessary for health that was published at the beginning of the 20th century, it was written: "…and instead of all of those, it is possible to use two teaspoonfuls of olive oil a day. All of the vitamins and all of the minerals necessary for health are found in olive oil."

n Europe, olive oil is used to prevent…
ear wax! All you do is drip two drops of
olive oil into the ear three times a day.

*N*atural medicine claims that olive oil is one of the best means for lowering the "bad" cholesterol level in the body and for preventing blood clots. Alternative medicine experts call the oil "the protector of cardiac health" because of its role in safeguarding the functioning of the heart.

*T*oday, herb-flavored olive oil can be purchased everywhere. It is flavored with various types of herbs, from basil to hot peppers. The herbs change the taste of the olive oil, so it is important to relate to the quality of the olive oil separately from the herbs. Herbs (especially if they're piquant) are liable to conceal the taste of low-grade olive oil.

hen high-quality olive oil is flavored with herbs, it can be stored under normal conditions for no longer than three or four months. Take note of the expiry date on the bottle!

*P*reparing herb-flavored olive oil is really easy. Fill one-third of a clean bottle or jar (it should be washed with hot water beforehand) with herbs according to taste, fill the bottle with high-quality olive oil, store in a cold, dark place (not in the refrigerator) and wait ten days. If you want piquant olive oil, change the herbs after 10 days and wait another ten days.

*I*t is very simple to change the flavor of the herb-flavored olive oil. Add a stronger herb than those in the original flavoring, wait ten days and use the oil. However, you can't tone down a piquant flavor.

*N*inety percent of the olive production in the world goes into the manufacture of olive oil, and only 10% of the olives, green or black, are eaten.

*T*he quality of the olives and the oil produced from them is influenced by the strain of olive (there are several dozen strains), by the place where they are grown, by the time when they are picked and by the weather conditions that prevail during the year.

*T*he olive-picking process largely determines the quality of the oil that is produced. The methods used are: manual picking, which preserves the wholeness of the olives (and safeguards the tree); beating the tree, whereby the olives fall onto sheets of fabric spread under the tree; and mechanical picking by means of machines that shake the tree; this method is at the bottom of the list.

*A*fter picking, the most important factor in determining the quality of the oil is the time that elapses between the picking and the beginning of oil production. The sooner the olives reach the olive press where the oil is extracted, the higher the quality of the oil. Private orchards make a point of ordering a press in advance, and transport the olives directly from the trees to the press in order to initiate the process.

A well-known Arab proverb says: "Olives that are not pressed [i.e., that have not had the oil extracted from them] on the day they are picked are like a bride whose husband does not come to her bed on her wedding night."

he oil-extracting process (after picking) in the press consists of three parts: (1) the olives are crushed into a black paste; (2) the "juice" is squeezed out of the paste – the juice being the oil (this process is called "cold pressing" because it does not involve any heating); (3) the  water from the olives that is present in the "juice" is separated off, and only the oil remains.

After the extraction of the oil by "cold pressing", various means, including heating, are used to produce olive oil of fairly low quality from the remaining mixture. This oil is mainly used for cooking.

Garlic and olive oil sauce

Ingredients:
12 unpeeled cloves of garlic
A handful of basil leaves
1 teaspoon Dijon mustard
1 teaspoon rosemary leaves
A pinch of ground chili pepper
A thick slice of white bread without the crust
Salt

Preparation:
Place all the ingredients except the olive oil in a
food processor. Process into a smooth mixture.
While the processor is operating, slowly pour the
olive oil in. Keep on processing until a smooth,
thick sauce is produced.

French olive spread

It is important to buy good olives and remove the pits, and under no circumstances those awful blackened ones.

Ingredients:
300g pitted black olives
3 anchovy fillets
2 teaspoons capers
2 peeled cloves of garlic
1 teaspoon of fresh thyme
Freshly ground black pepper
1 cup of high-quality olive oil

Preparation:
Place all the ingredients except the olive oil in a food processor. Process into a uniform (but not smooth) mixture. While the processor is operating, pour in a thin stream of olive oil. Spoon the spread into a jar and pour a little olive oil on top of it before closing the lid.

Spaghetti with garlic and olive oil

Ingredients (for four):

500 g spaghetti

1 cup delicately flavored olive oil

6-8 plump cloves of garlic, peeled and finely chopped

A pinch of crushed chili pepper

A bunch of parsley, chopped

Freshly ground black pepper

Salt

Preparation:
Cook the spaghetti al dente. In a big skillet, mix
the oil, the garlic and the chili, place the skillet
over medium heat and fry 2-3 minutes, until the
garlic begins to become golden.
Drain the pasta well and add to the sauce. Stir
over medium heat for a minute, using two
wooden spoons. Remove from the heat. Add the
parsley, season, and let the spaghetti rest for 2
minutes before serving.
Variations:
Add 1 cup toasted pine nuts along with the
parsley; fry 100 g chopped smoked goose breast
with the garlic; fry 50 g chopped sun-dried
tomatoes in oil with the garlic.

Goat cheese in olive oil

Ingredients:
500 g ripe, pungent goat cheese (St. Moore or
Valency, but feta or kashkaval can also be used)
A bunch of herbs (rosemary, thyme, sage, bay leaves)
1 teaspoon of coarsely broken black pepper
High-quality olive oil

Preparation:
Cut the blocks of cheese into cubes. Place all the
ingredients in a broad jar and cover with the oil. Store
in a dark, cool place. It is ready after a week and
keeps for a month.

Chemical tests determine three degrees of quality for olive oil. These are determined according to the percentage of acidity in the oil:

Extra virgin – less than 0.8% acidity. <u>This is the highest-quality oil.</u>
Fine virgin – less than 1.5% acidity.
Ordinary – less than 3% acidity.

t is important to remember a cardinal point regarding oil quality. The quality of the oil is determined by means of a chemical test, but the taste of the oil is determined by tasting (like wine), and, as we know, taste is an entirely personal thing.

hefs recommend keeping at least two types of olive oil in the kitchen: (1) olive oil with a delicate flavor that does not overpower other flavors in foods (generally not fried or cooked) whose flavors are "superficial"; and (2) olive oil with a strong flavor for foods that are fried and cooked.

*F*rying, cooking or roasting diminish the healthful properties of the oil. Cold olive oil added to cold salads, for instance, preserves all of its healthful properties.

*O*live oil that is stored in a dark bottle (usually green) and in a dark place, preserves its quality over time. Heat and direct light are the enemies of olive oil.

*T*he color of the oil actually has no bearing on its quality. Experts mention two colors for olive oil: (1) green olive oil, which is produced from green olives that did not ripen completely, and has a strong, potent flavor; and (2) yellowish olive oil, which is produced from ripe olives and has a delicate flavor.

 here the olive tree stops,
the Mediterranean ends.

(G. Duhamel)

*T*he ancient origins of the olive tree are not clear. Archeologists and botanists have found remains of olive trees and olive pits from before the Bronze Age, over 15,000 years ago. These remains are of wild olive trees, and they were all found in the Mediterranean basin.

he first evidence of the cultivation of olive trees was found in what is Syria today, on the border of Asia Minor of ancient times, and a great deal of evidence attesting to the cultivation of olive trees was found in Phoenicia and in the ancient Land of Israel in the period about 8,000 years ago (the Neolithic period).

*F*rom 6,000 BC, the cultivation of olive trees began to spread from the East (Syria and the Land of Israel) to the West – one branch spread to Egypt, Libya and Morocco of today as well as to southern Spain, and another branch passed through Turkey of today, reaching islands such as Crete and Sicily, and took over every good parcel of land in Greece, Italy, southern France and northern Spain. We can state that the nearer a piece of land is to the waters of the Mediterranean, the greater the chances of finding olive trees on it.

*T*he spread of the cultivation of olive trees via the two "branches" caused a division into the Phoenician branch – the southern branch – which spread via Egypt, Carthage and reached the Atlantic coast, and the northern, Greco-Roman branch, which spread along the Mediterranean shores of Europe.

*T*he cultivation of olive trees, the extraction of the oil and the oil trade between countries provide historians and archeologists with a broad basis for research on intercultural links. Oil was marketed in tall jars called amphoras, and these oil jars were transported from place to place. Their shards have been found in excavations. Thus, for instance, commercial documents (on clay tablets) dating from 4,000 years ago have been found. They

indicate deliveries of jars of oil from Ebla (in today's Syria) that are mentioned in numbers. Fragments of oil jars bearing the same numbers were found in the excavations at Knossos in Crete.

*I*n ancient Egypt, the olive tree carved out its niche during the fourth to sixth dynasties (between 4,000 and 4,500 years ago). There is a mention of sacred olive trees in Heliopolis under which the priests slept in order to make prophecies. Several hundred years later, the olive tree is mentioned in various papyri, the pharaohs were buried in sarcophagi upon which olive branches were carved, and popular beliefs ascribed magical powers as well as rejuvenating and aphrodisiac properties to olive oil.

37

*A*bout 3,500 years ago, the "cultured" olive tree reached Greece from Asia Minor. The Greeks went to Syria to learn about cultivating the olive tree and brought pressers over from Syria who taught them how to extract oil.

*A*ccording to the Roman tradition, King L. T. Priscus, known as "the old man" (a king in the mythological dynasty of the kings of Rome) brought the olive tree to Italy in the seventh century BC, and olive tree cultivation reached its peak in the third century AD. (Only the cultivation of vineyards exceeded it.)

he olive tree reached France (formerly Gallia) in the third century BC. According to tradition, Phocenses, who established the city that is known as Marseille today, brought olive seedlings with him from the East.

*I*n ancient times, the process of extracting oil – from crushing the olives to squeezing and pressing the paste and separating the oil from the water – was performed manually. Farmers and slaves would beat the olives with various instruments in order to extract the oil. During a certain period in Carthage, landowners had to prove that they had enough slaves before they could obtain the right to plant olive trees. Every 18 olive trees "required" one slave.

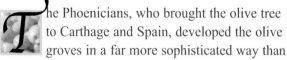he Phoenicians, who brought the olive tree to Carthage and Spain, developed the olive groves in a far more sophisticated way than the Greeks and the Romans. The Romans who conquered Carthage found olive groves that were hundreds of years old around it as well as a developed industry of olive oil extraction and trade. Olive trees arrived in Spain – mainly in the Andalusia region of today –  from Tunisia, and there were overseers who oversaw olive tree cultivation as early as the eighth century BC. During the same period, the cultivation of olive trees in Greece and Italy was still sporadic and irregular.

*I*n the third century BC, there was extensive export of oil from Andalusia to Rome. Special overseers indicated the origin, quality and aroma of the oil on every amphora.

*T*he Moslem conquest of Spain did nothing but good for the olive trees there. The Moslems planted olive trees until Andalusia looked (and still looks) like a forest of olive trees.

*F*rom the 16th century onward, the Spanish conquistadores took olive seedlings with them on their ships and planted them in the New World. The origin of olives in Mexico, Argentina, Peru, Chile and so on lies in those seedlings.

live trees reached the United States in the 18th century, when missionaries planted olive groves in California.

he Bible and the New Testament are full of references to the importance of the olive tree to mankind, from the dove that returned to Noah in the Ark with an olive branch in its beak to the Messiah whose Hebrew name comes from the action of anointing the head and the body with olive oil.

ccording to Greek mythology, Pallas Athena competed with Poseidon, god of the sea, for control of Athens. Poseidon offered the Athenians the horse, which could be used for work and riding. Pallas Athena made an olive tree grow in rocky ground, explaining that it gives shade and food and serves as a  medication for people. The council of the gods ruled that Pallas Athena had won the competition, and the city of Athens came under her patronage.

*H*omer mentions the olive tree, and it is obvious that he was well acquainted with its cultivation and uses. He writes: "This is the olive tree, which grows and stands tall, resists the fierce winds and burning sun, its flowers are white … and when the gale comes, its roots are torn from the ground and it is cast to the ground like a giant that is felled with one blow." And in fact, the olive tree grows in rocky ground in Greece, and for that reason, its roots are not deep and it is vulnerable when gales blow.

*A*ccording to the Bible, it is forbidden to cut down or destroy fruit-bearing olive trees, even if the olive tree belongs to the enemy. "Burn the city of the enemy, kill…people of the enemy… and do not raise your hand to the olive tree." were the warriors' instructions.

he Jews considered the olive tree to be "the king of trees" and believed that eating olives and drinking olive oil engendered wisdom and even enlightenment.

*L*et's not forget that Jesus Christ experienced his suffering at a place called Gethsemane (the place in which olive oil is produced) on the Mount of Olives.

n the Holy Qor'an of the Moslems, the olive tree and its fruit are mentioned hundreds of times.

*T*he dove with the olive branch, which began in Noah's ark and became famous in Picasso's paintings, is a symbol of peace to this day.

*T*he difference between olive oil and essential oils lies mainly in the production process. Olive oil is actually "juice" that is extracted mechanically by crushing and pressing. Essential oils are extracted by methods that include distillation at a high heat.

n the Middle Eastern region, in places where olive oil is the principal source of fat, the incidence of cardio-vascular diseases is extremely low. In the United States, where the main source of fat is saturated fat, the incidence of these diseases is extremely high.

*O*live oil contains absolutely no cholesterol.

Switching from consuming saturated fats to olive oil as a sole measure can work wonders lowering cholesterol levels.

n the Mediterranean region, olive oil serves as a substitute for fat in baking as well!

*O*live oil is used for frying. Although olive oil loses a large part of its properties in this process, it is still better than fat, and olive oil can be re-used for frying up to six times (as opposed to two or three times with regular oil), so that the difference in price balances out.

n a store that specializes in olive oils, you can find a selection of flavors, qualities and price ranges that is no smaller than in a store that specializes in wines.

he olive tree is an evergreen tree, and this fact is conspicuous in Mediterranean regions that are dry in the summer.

live trees are long-lived –
many of them yield fruit for
over 500 years.

*T*he olive tree yields fruit seven years after being planted. The number 7 is a "magic" number, and its link to the olive tree adds to the tree's good name.

ome billion olive trees are grown throughout the world.

*O*live oil maintains its quality much longer than other oils. In ideal storage conditions – a dark, cool place – olive oil maintains its quality for over three years.

*N*ow that the Americans have learned about the properties of olive oil, the import of olive oil into the United States has increased substantially in percentage in recent years.

*A*lmost all of the world's olive oil production is concentrated in the Mediterranean region. According to a conservative estimate, the average age of fruit-bearing olive trees in this region is 170 years.

*T*he flavor of the olive oil is determined by the color, the aroma, the fragrance, and so on. The quality of the olive oil from the same source or press, changes each year in accordance with the growing and picking conditions that prevailed during the particular year. Every ranking of "flavor" is a personal ranking, as with wine. The quality is determined according to the production process and chemical measures, and there is no doubt that oil that is defined as Extra Virgin Olive Oil is the best – and also the most expensive. It is the oil that is extracted from the first cold pressing of the olives.

*O*live oil experts and merchants define the flavors of olive oil in three categories: mild (delicate flavor), semi-fruity (subtle flavor of olive oil), and fruity (obvious taste of olive oil).

*T*he term cold pressing is a key term in the quality of olive oil. The olives are brought to the press where they are crushed, the paste is placed on a perforated surface, and the "juice" from the paste is collected in vats and separated into oil and water. Cold pressing is the first squeezing of this paste, which is done without any heating whatsoever.

live oil contributes about 10 calories per gram to your body (about 130 calories per teaspoonful).

*O*live oil is known to increase the amount of HDL (good cholesterol) in the body.

*E*xperts recommend that for cooking at high heat, roasting or frying, "olive oil" should be used (it contains mainly olive oil that was extracted by means of a process that includes heating); however, for seasoning or preparing cold dishes, or for drinking as is, **virgin** olive oil should be used.

n Lebanon, there is a village whose inhabitants drink a glass of olive oil in the morning and a glass of olive oil in the evening. The life-span of these people is 97 for men and 98 for women.

live oil is at its best at room
temperature. Olive oil that is
stored in the refrigerator looks
cloudy, but the cloudiness disappears when
the oil is stored at room temperature.

n the United States, one-fifth of all the olive oil sold is ranked as Extra Virgin Olive Oil. Quality wins!

*S*pain is the largest producer of olive oil in the world, and anyone who visits Spain notices that immediately. Some 40% of Spain's surface area is planted with olive trees. The bulk of the olive oil is produced in the Andalusia area. In Spain, there are four dominant types of olives: Cornicabra, Picual, Hojiblanca and Arbequina, the "Arab" olive.

*I*taly is the world's second most important producer of olive oil (about 2/3 of the amount produced by Spain). Most of the cultivation of olive trees occurs in southern Italy. The most common types of olives are: Moraiolo, Leccino, Frantoio and Coratina.

*G*reece, and especially the island of Crete, has the longest tradition of producing olive oil, but it is only the third largest producer. The most common type of olive is Koroneiki, which constitutes 100% of the olive trees in Crete. The olives of this strain are small but have a pungent aroma.

*T*unisia is an important producer of olive oil (about one-quarter of Spain's production) and exports olive oil to Europe and the Far East. In Tunisia, olive trees grow on the desert border.

*I*n Turkey, there is extensive cultivation of olive trees of the Memecik strain, but the production of olive oil is low (about half of what Tunisia produces). This is because in Turkey, the consumption of olives is widespread, and most of the crop is consumed as olives and not as oil.

*P*ortugal, Spain's neighbor, cultivates olive trees and imports… olive oil from Spain and Tunisia. Portugal is considered to be a country in which the consumption of olive oil per person is the highest, and despite its own production, the country has to import olive oil from its neighbors.

orocco is the sixth largest producer of olive oil, and its leaders hope that in coming years its ranking will improve.

*F*rance, especially in the south, also cultivates olive trees. Most of the crop is used for local consumption, either as olives or as olive oil.

*I*n the United States, olive trees are raised primarily for the production of olives for consumption. The most common strains of olives there are Manzanillo and Gordal, which are only used for eating, and Mission (planted by the Franciscan missionaries in California), which are also used for the production of olive oil.

*I*n Argentina, the olive trees mainly produce olives for consumption, but today there is government support for the production of olive oil. Argentina's climate and broad expanses of land are good for it.

*I*srael cultivates olive trees mainly for the production of olives for eating (the Manzanillo strain, as in the United States), but also for the production of olive oil. The quality of the oil is good, but the amounts extracted are small.

*T*he label on the bottle of olive oil features several terms with which every buyer should be familiar. They are as follows:

Extra Virgin Olive Oil – unanimously acclaimed as the best oil.

Virgin Olive Oil – Second best after "Extra", but still excellent olive oil, which is produced in the same way (without heating) and is excellent for cooking, even at high temperatures.

Lampante Olive Oil – In fact, this is olive oil "in process" – olive oil whose acidity is above 3%, or oil that was flawed in production or storage, or oil from a poor crop. This oil undergoes chemical processes of refining and can return to the market with names such as "Pure Olive Oil" or "Refined Olive Oil" or even "Extra Light Olive Oil."

First Cold Pressed – This is olive oil that is
produced by mechanical means in a primary
process of crushing – pressing and separating the
olive oil from the water, and all this at a
temperature identical to that of the human body.

Acidity – This is the chemical measure used for determining the quality of the olive oil. The lower the level of acidity is, the higher the quality of the olive oil. Gourmets should ensure that the acidity is 0.3% or less!

Extra Light Olive Oil – This is an American term that hints at fewer calories but is actually olive oil that has been refined.

Olive-Pomace Oil – This is olive oil that is produced from the remains of the first paste (mainly pits and skin) by means of a heating process. It is cheap olive oil that is mainly used for cooking.

*A*bout 25 million acres of land are cultivated with olive trees worldwide – most of them in the Middle East, Europe and North Africa. In massive China, there are only 2,000 acres of olive trees.

ittle Cyprus produces twice the amount of olive oil as the enormous United States.

*O*live oil is the perfect remedy for treating dry skin, cracked skin or a rash on the skin (in the latter case, a physician should be consulted as well). Spreading olive oil over the skin stimulates the regeneration of damaged cells.

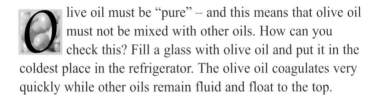

live oil must be "pure" – and this means that olive oil must not be mixed with other oils. How can you check this? Fill a glass with olive oil and put it in the coldest place in the refrigerator. The olive oil coagulates very quickly while other oils remain fluid and float to the top.

ccording to a well-known Arab proverb, the person who brings his olives "from the tree to the stone" will become very wealthy. This means that olives must be picked from the tree (not gathered from the ground) and brought directly to the millstone that crushes them.

*P*eople who are meticulous about gathering olives use straw baskets or wooden crates. Gathering olives in sacks causes the olives to cave in and smell moldy. Experts claim that the quality of virgin olive oil declines by one degree (out of 10) for every two hours that the olives are in sacks.

*T*he best time for picking olives from the tree for oil extraction is after three days of rain. (The olives swell a bit and it is easier to pick them; the excess water is separated from the oil during pressing.) Rainless days cause the olives to fall to the ground.

n Mediterranean countries, they say that the best time to pick olives is when they're purple – that is, during the transition from green to black.

*A*n important factor in the quality of the oil is the quality of the fruit, the olive, and an important factor in the quality of the olive is… the prevalence of olive flies! These flies bite the olives, lay their eggs and diminish its quality because of the large worms in the olive. Spraying the leaves against olive flies prevents damage like this to the olives.

 at olives and anoint yourselves with their oil since the olive is the blessed tree of the Prophet Muhammed, the prophet of Islam.

n the Middle East, the cure for every illness is… two teaspoons of olive oil with a teaspoon of bee honey.

If a baby or child has a cold, rubbing olive oil into his chest and back will make him better immediately. The olive oil is rubbed in before sleeping, and the child should be snugly covered with a sheet or shirt.

*O*live oil is rubbed into fresh wounds or onto dry scabs, and this promotes the regeneration of the skin and reduces the size of the permanent scars.

A sore back is cured after a massage with olive oil. Tried and tested!

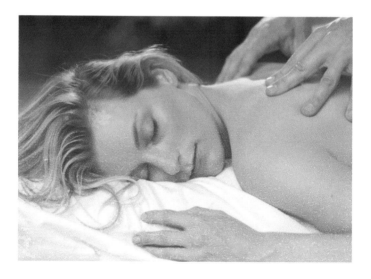

Soap that is based on olive oil is thought to prevent hair loss. Olive-oil soap is a by-product of oil extraction, and olives that were gathered from the ground or damaged during harvesting are used in the production process.

oiling) olive oil was a terrifying weapon in ancient times. Josephus Flavius relates that the inhabitants of Yodfat in the Galilee (a place where olives grew in abundance) poured boiling olive oil onto the Romans who were besieging the city.

n the hot regions of the Mediterranean, olives are picked during the early morning hours when they are still cool. Olives that have absorbed the heat of the sun tend to become moldy after the harvest.

n the process of oil production, the last stage is the one in which the crushed olives are placed in small baskets, and by means of a pestle, the paste is squeezed in order to press the liquids out of it. The remaining substance, olive waste, is used for the production of "industrial"

olive oil (after heating) or as a high-quality combustible substance for ovens. Fancy bakeries buy olive waste in order to fuel their bread-baking ovens, and this imbues the bread with a special flavor.

A group of archeologists who uncovered an olive press in Syria learned just how similar the process of extracting olive oil today is to what it was thousands of years ago, in the times of King David and Jesus: a week after they had left the site, the locals began to use the ancient press to extract olive oil!

*A*nd the dove came in to him in the evening; and, lo, in her mouth was an olive leaf pluckt off: so Noah knew that the waters were abated from off the earth.

GENESIS, Chap. 8, 11

ow when Jesus was in Bethany, in the house of Simon the leper, There came unto him a woman having an alabaster box of very precious ointment [olive oil], and poured it on his head, as he sat at meat. But when his disciples saw it, they had indignation, saying, To what purpose is this waste? For this ointment might have been sold for much, and given to the poor. When Jesus understood it,

he said unto them, Why trouble ye the woman? For she hath wrought a good work upon me. For ye have the poor always with you; but me ye have not always. For in that she hath poured this ointment on my body, she did it for my burial. Verily I say unto you, Wheresoever this gospel shall be preached in the whole world, there shall also this, that this woman hath done, be told for a memorial of her.

MATTHEW, Chap. 26, 6-13

 nd they cast out many devils, and anointed with oil many that were sick, and healed them.

MARK, Chap. 6, 13

*F*or if thou wert cut out of the olive tree which is wild by nature, and wert graffed contrary to nature into a good olive tree: how much more shall these, which be the natural branches, be graffed into their own olive tree?

ROMANS, Chap. 11, 24

or if the firstfruit be holy, the lump is also holy: and if the root be holy, so are the branches. And if some of the branches be broken off, and thou, being a wild olive tree, wert graffed in among them, and with them partakest of the root and fatness of the olive tree; Boast not against the branches. But if thou boast, thou bearest not the root, but the root thee.

ROMANS, Chap. 11, 16-18

Coffee

A cultural history from around the world

Ed S. Milton

9654941589

Tea

A cultural history from around the world

Ed S. Milton

9654941597

Olive Oil

A cultural history from around the world

Ed S. Milton

9654941600

Wine

A cultural history from around the world

Ed S. Milton

9654941619